Sis, Heal

The Barnes Sisters

Library of Congress Cataloging-in-Publication Data

The Barnes Sisters, Victorian Barnes and Francine Barnes
Sis, Heal
Published by: Billionaire Barnes, LLC

ISBN 978-1-7344444-0-7

10 9 8 7 6 5 4 3 2 1

Printed in the United States of America

Note: This book is intended only as a real-life testimony of the life and times of The Barnes Sisters. Readers are advised to consult a professional before making any changes in their life. The reader assumes all responsibility for the consequences of any actions taken based on the information presented in this book. The information in this book is based on the author's research and experience. Every attempt has been made to ensure that the information is accurate; however, the author cannot accept liability for any errors that may exist. The facts and theories about life are subject to interpretation, and the conclusions and recommendations presented here may not agree with other interpretations.

We dedicate this book to Francine Barnes' beautiful children, Davont'e Jr., Divine, Dream, and Victorian Barnes' future children. May our healing process break the toxic generational curses you would have inherited.

To every person who has hurt us, we forgive you.

Contents

Introduction

Sis, you need to heal. While we do not know you personally, we understand you are currently hurting from past or present emotional pain. Instead of allowing pain to hinder your life's progression, we invite you to begin your intentional, healing journey with us by reading this book.

Sis, Heal is the story of how we, The Barnes Sisters, transformed our inherited pain into purpose. It captures traumatic events we endured from birth through adulthood to encourage you to identify those things, events, or people that have emotionally scarred your own life. Every woman (and person, in general) has undergone some level of pain in her life and encompasses the choice of healing. Healing is necessary in order to break through to higher levels of living. Once we became aware of multiple generational curses over our lives, we began to think and move differently so that our current and future children would never experience the life of poverty, homelessness, abandonment, abuse and chaos we endured.

We believe that everything that has happened to us over the years, positive and negative, has served a greater purpose for our lives. Even in pain, we would always reassure ourselves that nothing we were currently experiencing would be in vain. We always knew we would overcome. And here we are today, telling our story filled with the actions of people who hurt us, mistakes we've made, pain we've gone through, and steps we either took or are beginning to take towards healing. We have made an intentional decision to transform our pain into purpose and we invite you to do the same, sis. Our hope is that you will feel empowered towards living out your life's purpose as a healed woman. We are excited for you! Begin your journey with The Barnes Sisters, now.

Background

The Barnes Sisters were raised identically, yet their journeys through adolescence and adulthood took opposite turns. While Victorian Barnes, the older sister, channeled her childhood pain into improving the quality of her life, Francine Barnes temporarily succumbed to the pressures of her toxic environment. Ultimately, a series of divine, yet painful events brought them back together to begin the journey towards healing from their traumatic past while striving towards a purpose-filled future.

Their earlier years were plagued with homelessness, abandonment, and sexual abuse. The last of their mother's eight children, The Barnes Sisters experienced a level of struggle uncommon to anyone else in their family. Born in Chicago, Illinois, their mother arrived to Oakland, California at the age of five years old with her parents and seven siblings. Although her parents were devoted Christians, she grew up in a very abusive household and never got to witness what healthy, real love looked like. She only knew how unhealthy, toxic love felt. Eventually, the Barnes Sisters' mother got married and had her first two sons by the age of 19. Not long after her second son was born, her husband left her to raise the two boys on her own. Over the next few years, she conceived a son and three daughters by her second husband. As a mother of 6 kids by the age of 32, she had never allowed herself time to heal from her painful past. She became a single mother again, when her drug-addicted husband abandoned his family. Even with the support of her parents, it was hard for her to maintain an orderly household for her kids, but she provided the basic necessities for a comfortable life. Early on, she instilled them with the power of faith. She loved the Lord and lived to please Him. The dynamics of her family changed when she began to struggle with thyroid disease. She was no longer able to provide a safe home for 6 kids so she moved in with her mother. Then, she met another man. He was intelligent and had a passion for computers. He was also a smooth talker. Although they never got married, they eventually conceived two girls. . . . The Barnes Sisters.

CHAPTER 1

Overcoming Childhood Trauma

Part I

As a mother, imagine bringing a seventh child into the world, without a place to call your own home. You've just given birth to a healthy baby girl and upon release from the hospital, you and the baby join your six other kids and a few relatives in your mother's living room. You currently receive government financial assistance every month, but it doesn't cover all of your family's basic needs. For the last year, several family members have welcomed you into their homes for a short period of time but, essentially, you and your children are homeless.

I, Victorian Barnes, was born in Oakland, California, the seventh of eight children. Prior to my birth, my family moved around a bit, but for the most part, experienced a decent quality of life. After my mother's thyroid disease drastically overtook her physical well-being, my siblings began to feel the discomfort of unstable living. My mother tried to keep her family together, but my brothers eventually separated from her and my sisters to live with other relatives.

During the first year of my life, my mother, three sisters, and I lived in my grandmother's small two-bedroom high-rise apartment. Eventually, we moved into my father's home. Although I was the only child he had with my mother at the time, (he also had another daughter from his previous wife) he provided for the entire household and treated all my siblings as if they were his own children. He was very present and active to me and my siblings, as he helped with homework, treated us well, and spoiled us with our favorite treats. When I was one years old, we welcomed my mother's last child, Francine Barnes, into our family. Over the next year, my family started to witness a different side of my father. He became very controlling and aggressive. We never knew it at the time but my father was heavily addicted to alcohol and possibly, drugs. He loved all of us in the ways he knew how to show love; however, one argument between my parents eventually led to my family being homeless again. My father kicked his two biological infant children, my mother, and two sisters out of his home. Now, we were back to being crammed in our grandmother's living room.

We moved around to different relatives' homes for years. Many days, we stayed in hotel rooms. On rare occasions, we slept in public spaces throughout the nights. While I do not recall the details around the first four or five years of my life, I remember the events that took place in one particular uncle's living room very vividly. When I was five years old, my older male cousin would occasionally supervise me and Fanny while everyone else was out of the apartment. We hated him since he would always torture us.

Round and around he swung us by our skinny little arms and then suddenly, let us go, sending us flying across the room crying. Even worse, he would take us one by one, between the refrigerator door and force us to perform oral sex on him. Yes, at the young age of four and five, Fanny and I were introduced to sex. I am not sure how many times we were sexually abused but I remember no longer feeling like the innocent little girl I once was. At a very young age, we became interested in sex by watching pornographic videos and magazines. I recall various times we tried to re-enact what we saw, on each other. Being homeless was bad enough; the molestation completely ruined my childhood. However, I still thrived.

I never allowed any struggles from home to interfere with my school work since I've always loved learning new things. I remember leading my classroom as one of the top academic achievers, through-out elementary school and beyond. I was also very well-behaved. Not many people outside of family knew about the challenges I faced at home. However, my teachers grew highly concerned when I consistently missed one or two days from school each week. I was typically the last student to arrive to class and the last to leave. One day, I remember being sent to the office after waiting for my mother to come pick me up from school. I heard my principal discussing the option of calling Child Protective Services. Tears streaming down my eyes, I went outside to the front of the school to see if my mom was there yet. From afar, I could see my grandmother pacing down the street. I was so relieved as I ran into her arms. She took me home.

When I was eight years old, my family moved into a four-bedroom apartment. We were so happy to finally have a place to call our own! Each sister had her own room; Fanny and I shared one. I believe my mother slept in the living room, although I do not remember seeing her there as much. My mom had a job at the time, but still struggled to provide basic necessities for the household. Many days, we did not have hot water, electricity, nor food to eat. We typically bathed with cold water, used candles or propane heaters, and depended on my older sisters to bring in hot food from their jobs. Fanny and I slept on air beds in our empty room and used storage bins as dressers. Nonetheless, we enjoyed creating fun, unforgettable moments together as a family. Then one day, the inevitable occurred. We came home from school to find an eviction notice on the door. We found out that my mother had not been paying the rent. We always wondered where her money was going each month since we were not seeing much fruit from her labor. Now, the little we had was locked away inside our apartment. We broke in through the back door to place as many items as we could into trash bags. Since my mother wasn't able to keep her sons together with the family, she tried her best to maintain a home for her girls.

But after getting evicted and being left homeless again, we all were forced to go separate ways. My mother, Fanny, older sister, and I continued to move around from living room to living room all the way through my middle school years.

Living in unstable environments throughout my childhood caused me to suffer in many ways as a teenager and adult. Chaos and instability became normal to me. Although I had faith, I lacked important values and teachings to guide me through life. However, I did not allow my ignorance to hinder me. I became very independent and took the responsibility of making the right decisions into my own hands. I sought out physical and virtual guidance about life from outside mentors and coaches. I was motivated to push myself towards greatness. It would have been easy to become a victim of my circumstances. I was homeless, poor, abandoned, and sexually molested before the age of 10. Yet, I still found a way to excel by allowing my unfortunate circumstances to develop a high level of resilience within me. It may have seemed as if I were born to lose but in fact, I was being set up to win all along.

Part II

The black sheep. The wild child. Due to the life decisions I made during my adolescent years, those were the labels I had received while growing up, which set me apart from Vickey and my other older siblings. Ironically, being the youngest of eight children seemed as if it came with a blessing and a curse. My mother was 38 when she birthed me. You would think that after 7 kids, years of homelessness and welfare, she would have considered getting her tubes tied. She had her first child at 17 and spent the next 3 decades birthing and raising kids without the consistent help from any of her children's fathers.

Growing up, I silently praised my mom for her presence. She was a strong woman in my eyes because I never heard her complain about the responsibilities that came with being a single, struggling mother. My father, on the other hand, was absent more than he was present and I shamed him for it. I resented him for his inability to be the man I desperately needed to guide me through every moment in my life. I couldn't understand why he didn't view fatherhood as his first priority. His absence was silent but it felt so loud. Although my memory from my childhood is vague, I knew I was the epitome of a girl being raised without her father's constant presence. The resentment I had for him grew stronger as I got older. All those years, I painted him as the villain in my life. My mother was my hero; a savior for her children. It wasn't until my teenage years and adulthood that I realized my mother's presence came with a level of pain that seemed to have as much of an effect on me as my father's absence.

My father introduced my mother to gambling and she eventually became addicted, which made our unstable living situation worse when we were evicted for delinquent rent. I remember when my mother would come up to my school every first of the month before heading off to the casinos. Those visits were bittersweet because although I was happy to see her, I knew the reason for her unexpected appearance. She would fill my backpack with snacks for me to take home, since she knew she'd disappear for the next few days or even weeks. Out of all the countless times she temporarily left the state to gamble, I could only remember her coming back one time with more money than she initially left with. How ironic was it for her to be heavily addicted to something she had no luck at? All the other times, she would come back completely broke and crying, expressing her sorrow for leaving us over and over again. We always forgave her, not fully understanding the depths of the consequences her actions were causing us. As time passed, her gambling addiction began to subside once I graduated from elementary school. Although she never fully quit, she started going less and less.

Despite all the dysfunction I was dealing with, I still managed to be one of the top students in my elementary and middle school classes. School was like a safe haven for me; an escape from the turmoil I was dealing with at home. Middle school offered a different environment from what I was accustomed to since I attended a predominantly African-American middle school in 6th grade. Transitioning from an Asian elementary school to an African-American school was a bit uncomfortable for me but I adjusted pretty well.

I was in the 6th grade when I met my first love, during the middle of the year. I was 11 and he was 12. He was a well-known nuisance in school, while I was the smart, yet quiet little girl. I don't know if opposites attracted or if he wanted me to be his girlfriend because he thought I would do his homework but either way, what was supposed to be a middle school fling turned into something much deeper than we both expected over the next decade. Growing up without my father and 3 older brothers around for guidance, I allowed him to fill a void in my life that I didn't know existed at the time. We both unknowingly shared similar dysfunctions that life unwillingly handed us. Over the years, we became close. He was someone I felt I could trust with my heart.

I was 13 years old when I lost my virginity to him. Experiencing sex for the first time made me feel like I had become a woman that night. My innocence died and the beginning of an uncontrollable rebellion was born. I walked back to my big sister's apartment replaying what had just happened. Although my mother wasn't the interrogating type, I was still hoping she wouldn't sense anything different about me. Luckily, my sister Vickey wasn't home at the time. We shared the same room and I didn't want her questioning me. I wanted to keep the love I had just experienced sacred between my first love and I. That night I felt genuinely loved by a man for the first time in 13 years.

I grew up viewing love as an inconsistent act by the way my father periodically came in and out of my life. I felt abandoned by him because he wasn't present enough to give me the masculine love my soul yearned for. I was experiencing life without the proper love and guidance I needed, which caused me to make continuous mistakes in my early teenage years. Those mistakes resulted in me being left with permanent emotional and mental scars. Based upon my mistakes, my life appeared to be on a path towards destruction. As I got older, I understood that according to God's plan, my life was destined for greatness from the very beginning.

Reflection

*W*hat was your childhood and adolescent years like? Did you experience extreme hardships like us? Or was it stable and peaceful? Who or what events had the greatest impact on your life during those years? Our childhood and teenage years play a huge role in the way we view and move throughout our adulthood. Many of our current values, ideas, and motivations have stemmed from what we've seen and experienced as a child, without us even knowing. Our adolescent years are where we become more easily influenced and shaped by our surroundings. Reflect on all the experiences of your youth that shaped the woman you are today. If you've experienced trauma, allow those memories to fuel your motivations for creating a life that is completely different from what you've experienced. Do not repeat traumatizing cycles. Your future family is depending on you!

Create a solid action plan on the life you want to create for your kids or yourself. You had no control over what happened to you as a child. Now that you're an adult, you are in complete control of the actions, attitude, and effort you put forward in your own life. Your toxic childhood is no longer an excuse to remain where you are. In order to heal from your past, it's important to reflect back on your life to gain an understanding of where your pain originated from. Instead of living life hurt, confront your pain and grow from it. Sis, heal.

CHAPTER 2

Discovering Soul Ties

Part I

Exposing myself to unprotected sex at an early age was one of the biggest mistakes I made. I had never received the sex talk from my mother or my older siblings growing up and was oblivious to the fact that my actions could have led to irreversible consequences - like an unexpected teen pregnancy or an STD. As I began having unprotected sex with my first love more frequently, my focus towards building our relationship increased. Eventually, my irresponsible actions began to hinder my ability to remain focused in school. Life was moving at a speed faster than I could handle or even understand.

By sophomore year of high school, my life seemingly took a drastic turn in the wrong direction. With minimal rules being enforced by my mother, I began making poor decisions and my ability to thrive under pressure diminished. As I began to seek an escape from reality, my first love was there to provide me with something that I felt was missing - unconditional love and attention. However, I never expressed how chaotic my life was to him during that time. It wasn't until he had been stabbed by a close family member and months later shot by a random individual, that I became aware of how chaotic his life was, as well. His ability to show me love even while dealing with his own trauma caused me to grow a love for him deeper than I had ever felt for any man, including my father. With time, I allowed him to slowly gain control over my heart, my mind and my body.

After getting into trouble and spending a few months in jail, he was ordered to move to Texas and live with his father upon release. His departure impacted my life tremendously. Now in different states, our emotions began to shift and we were incapable of maintaining a long-distance relationship. No matter what, I knew who my heart belonged to; I wanted to be with him and I was willing to do any and everything to make it happen.

As my mother got older, she became more lenient in her parenting with Vickey and I. At age 15, I was able to easily convince her that I was spending spring break at a friend's house when, in fact, I flew to Texas to spend the week with my first love. I had stolen money from my older sister to purchase a plane ticket. A year later, I ventured on a second trip to Texas with the intention of never coming back. With so much turmoil occurring in my life, being in Texas with my first love was the only place I felt accepted. I packed the few items that I owned in a suitcase and left to the airport. When I arrived in Texas, he was there to welcome me with open arms. Eventually, everyone found out about me running away but at the moment, I didn't care.

Despite my family's disapproval, I was finally happy and didn't have any desire to leave. He had his own business, apartment, car, and money - I was comfortable with the idea of staying. He was willing to take care of me and provide a life different from the unstable one I was living in California. While there, he slowly began grooming me on how to become a "wife" at the age of 16. He taught me how to cook, clean, and I was willingly having sex on demand. With his guidance, I even attempted to enroll in high school and get my first job. I was appreciative of his willingness to utilize his time instilling different things within me. Although, I wasn't quite ready for the things he was trying to teach me, I obliged not wanting to disappoint him.

Everything was going smooth until the unexpected occurred. For the first time ever, he hit me! Angered by something minor I had done, he slapped me with full force. I held my burning face as I fell to the ground, looking up at him in total shock. It was one of my most traumatizing experiences. How could the first man that ever showed me genuine love, be the first man to hit me? The same hands he used to caress me were the ones he abused me with. I cried uncontrollably while he apologized, holding me, telling me he'd never do it again. I forgave him. I couldn't understand how my love for him grew deeper after that. This incident was the beginning of my refined perspective of love since I begin to correlate love with pain.

After 4 weeks of my brother threatening to call the police, it was time for me to leave Texas. Half of me dreaded the departure and the other half was anxious to be back with my mother. Clearly, I still possessed the soul of a little girl in spite of the adult decisions I was making. I finally arrived back to California and to my surprise, I was pregnant! Yes, 16 and pregnant; the first in my family to hold that title. My mother felt like she had failed me. Everyone in my family blamed my first love. I always wondered whether he was really the one to blame or was my lack of sufficient parenting the reason my life had spiraled out of control. With my first love being overjoyed at the thought of being a father and my mother being disappointed at the thought of her baby girl becoming a mother, I didn't know how to feel. I was torn between the decision on whether I should continue on with the pregnancy or get an abortion.

After spending 11 weeks in fear of being disowned by my family and lack of support from my mother, I got an abortion. My mother practically forced me to make this decision, so I felt there wasn't much I could do. The abortion was a two-day process. The first day, I went to get laminaria inserted into my cervix to get my body ready for the surgical procedure that was going to take place the next day. Although my body was ready to endure the removal of my unborn seed, there was nothing I could do to prepare my mind for what was about to occur.

Too scared and ashamed to tell my first love the truth, I lied and told him I had miscarried. Deep down, he knew I aborted our baby. It seemed as though his love for me died right along with his unborn seed. I hurt him, and there was nothing I could do to redeem myself. Trying to seek comfort, I went to his grandmother's house since that was the only place I felt accepted at the moment. I had become overwhelmed with emotions of trying to cope with the abortion in addition to my unstable living conditions. I called my first love crying, expressing how abandoned I felt. He rejected me. Feeling helpless, I went into the kitchen, grabbed the sharpest knife in the drawer and attempted to cut my wrist. His grandmother ran in behind me and held me down, trying to console me while removing the knife from my hand. In spite of my attempts to harm myself, he was still hurt by my actions and his heart remained cold as he told me to leave his grandmother's house and never come back. That was the end of our relationship and friendship. I was left alone to cope with the abortion my mother forced me to have. A part of me died right along with the death of my unborn seed.

Part II

As a high-school student, I continued to excel in the classroom. I became very resourceful and seized opportunities geared towards bettering myself and future. One of the best decisions I made during my teenage years was joining two college preparatory programs for disadvantaged minorities. Through free continued education, extracurricular activities, mentorship, tutoring, and employment opportunities, I finally figured out how I would escape the plight of homelessness and poverty. At the age of 15, I began preparing for college. I would be only the second of my mother's eight children to attend a four-year university. Over the next few years, mentors and educators within these two college prep programs became the supportive family I never had. They poured positive energy and knowledge into all areas of my life, helping me make better life decisions. They also held me accountable in maintaining good grades by requesting them each semester. One of my mentors would actually go a step further and check up on me in class, every now and then. When I wasn't working at jobs my programs offered or volunteering with different organizations, I attended weekly workshops and classes. I was so focused on bettering my life to the point I rarely spent time at my sister's house, which is where my mother, Fanny, and I were staying at the time.

But I was far from the perfection I was portraying to others. I began trying activities my peers engaged in, like smoking weed and getting drunk and eventually, sex with my first and only boyfriend I had during those years. I met him while riding the bus home one evening. He asked for my number before I got off and after a few phone conversations, we made things official. Over the next year and a half, we developed a bond through spending quality time together, hours of conversing about our lives and even getting to know each other's families. He was a hood dude, but I loved him for always being available with time and attention I yearned for. Prior to him, I had never felt loved by a man. He was not good to me, though. He lied about his whereabouts, and different girls started claiming him as their man. Worse enough, he went to jail, but I continued to communicate with him through phone calls and letters. Once he got out, I agreed to store an illegal gun for him in my bedroom closet. What was I thinking? One day, as he expressed how good I was to him and how no other woman would put up with him, I realized I deserved better. So, right on the spot, I broke up with him. The next day, he was sitting on the living room couch as I came out of my bedroom; I kicked him out and continued to let him know that our relationship was over. We spoke on the phone every now and then but never got back together. The puppy love I had for him instantly began to fade away, as I thought about how the first boy I ever loved hurt me.

Part III

I was forced to continue life without my first love's guidance, love, or attention. My family had temporarily shut me out, as I continued making poor decisions that drug me further down the destructive path I was already on. I barely attended school and on the days I did go, I arrived hours late. There was no one in my corner to motivate me. I was no longer living in the same household as my mother or Vickey. Since no one trusted me to be in their home without stealing from them, I moved from house to house. I slowly began to feel like I had no purpose in life. My mother couldn't help me since she could barely help herself. My father knew about my living situation and still decided to close his doors on me. I felt rejected by everyone around me.

As junior year of high school approached, my older brother eventually took me into his home, since I had nowhere else to go. His stable home was an environment unfamiliar to me. I had my own room, my own bed, and generally my own space; but I couldn't find comfort since dysfunction had become normal to me. He tried to reshape my foundation and give me structure because he knew I didn't receive a proper upbringing. To escape the discomfort, I rebelled against the positive change of stability he was seeking for my life. By that time, I had experienced so much trauma and had no desire to change. Ultimately, I was too unmanageable for my brother during that time so living with him didn't last very long. I went back to living unstable, going from house to house. It wasn't until my adult years where I recognized and appreciated my brother for the effort he put into reshaping my identity.

During this time, I felt I needed attention; yet there was nobody around to give me what I was seeking. Fully aware of this, I began to shift my focus towards different men that seemed to take an interest in me. I wanted affection, even if it was temporary. I needed to feel loved, even if it wasn't real. I was vulnerable and everywhere I went, men sensed it - all the wrong ones. I started to meet many men, mostly older ones, who were willing to give me what I had been missing in my life during that time. I gave them my body, using sex as a way to cope with the voids and distract me from the pain I was feeling. With different men, came different sexual encounters. 2 body counts turned into 3, and 3 turned into 4. I was engaging in unprotected sex without weighing the consequences of my actions.

I met the majority of the men while I stood at the bus stop on my way to school, while they drove by in their cars. One particular time, a man in his late 30's offered to give me a ride to school after a few moments of us conversing. My past had birthed a fearless girl so it was easy to accept a ride from a complete stranger. I knew that ride came with a price and at 16, the only thing I had to offer was my body. I was practically homeless, living at my sister's house, sleeping in my niece's room on the floor. I wasn't going to reject anybody that opened their home to me. I began having sex with him within a few nights of being at his house.

There were occasions when these men would take me to a hotel room instead of their homes. In a weird way, part of my body desired sex and intimacy, while the other part dreaded every moment of intercourse we had. As I reflect back on one of my most traumatic sexual encounters, I can still remember tasting the bitterness in his mouth when our tongues intertwined while kissing. I remember the way my body tensed up as he climbed on top of me and inserted his 40 year old penis into my underaged vagina. In the moment, my body was being satisfied but when he finally ejaculated, I felt relieved that it was over. Showers couldn't cleanse the filth that embedded my skin while he laid on top of me naked with sweat dripping from his chest onto my body, seeping into my pores. How was this man so comfortable having sex with a minor? I use to wonder how my father would feel if he knew his baby girl was having sex with men his age.

With time came more temporary men. 4 bodies eventually turned into 5, 6, and 7; sex became riskier. I was willing to have sex anywhere, from trap houses to public parks. These men were predators, and I was everything they were looking for to have a good time -- provocative, spontaneous, and most obvious, lost.

Drained from the fast lifestyle I was living, I became eager to engulf myself with something productive. I began searching for a job. I applied and started my first job at McDonalds. Although I was still in school, my job helped temporarily distract my mind from men, but working there made it harder to resist the different ones that came in and out during my shifts. A few appeared to be genuinely kindhearted but it was evident that most only wanted one thing - sex.

After meeting and exchanging numbers with one particular guy I met at work, my promiscuity almost cost me my life. After a brief conversation, we arranged to meet later that evening; he picked me up from my brother's apartment. I was dressed in all black and barely clothed in skimpy shorts, a shirt that only covered my breast along with 6 inch heels. We drove to his house and I sat in the car while he went inside. A few minutes later, he came back to the car but his demeanor had changed; he had a small handgun and another male with him. As I began talking to him, he started yelling and demanding that I be quiet. I sat in the front seat confused and shaken with fear. As we pulled into the gas station, I used that opportunity to escape immediately. I opened the door and jumped out of the car, running away as fast as I could. Luckily, my brother's friend was at the gas station and witnessed what had just occurred. Without hesitation, he told me to get in his car, reassuring me he'd transport me safely back to my brother's apartment.

Needing someone to confide in, I called a friend to inform him on what had just happened. During that call, I found out that he was familiar with the guy who had just tried to harm me. At that moment, I cried as he explained how the guy could have potentially taken my life. He was given bad drugs years prior to our encounter, and was well-known for having sporadic, uncontrollable, and dangerous behavior. By God's protection and grace, I knew I was blessed to be alive.

Before I knew it, I had engaged in sex with a total of 11 men, from 18-60 years old, over the course of a year. The men I exchanged my body with had begun to take a toll on my life - I had created dangerous soul ties. My promiscuity eventually came to an end after meeting a man most would consider a pedophile - he was 63 years old, while I was 17. We met as he watched me get kicked out of my sister's apartment for having an argument with my brother-in- law. That night, as I was left with nowhere to go, he offered to pay for my hotel room. Being young and naive, I viewed his behavior as an act of compassion, instead of realizing how he preyed on my vulnerability. Ultimately, out of all the men I had dealt with, besides my first love, he was the one that became the most beneficial. He provided me with money, support and some form of stability. He gave me the attention I wanted and made me feel loved because of his concern for my well-being. He became my sugar daddy.

Fed up with the constant instability of not having a comfortable place to call home, I began seeking help. Most of the programs that offered assistance were only available to those who were 18 and older. With my current situation, I felt I couldn't wait until I was 18. I needed help immediately. After careful research, I found out I would be eligible to receive help if I became emancipated. I didn't hesitate to start the paperwork. When I told my mother about the option of being emancipated, she cried. She felt like she had failed me, again. Without much hesitation, she signed the papers, signing over her rights to have guardianship control over me. She knew she was no longer capable of taking care of me. I had legally become an adult at 17.

By that time, I had fallen so far behind in school that I had to enroll in a continuing education school. At 17, I was living out of hotels, working at McDonalds, and attending school on a consistent basis. Despite my living arrangements, things were finally starting to flow at a steady pace for me. Eventually, the time came for me to give him something in return. He wanted sex and I didn't hesitate to give it to him; I couldn't afford to lose him. I wanted to make sure he was satisfied so that I could continue receiving the support I desperately needed from him.

As graduation approached, he made sure I was attending school every day. Dropping me off and picking me up had become a part of his daily routine. He didn't have a job; he was a hustler, so he always had time to be there for me when I needed him. The week before my graduation day, he paid for my senior portraits and took me to the mall to purchase the dress and heels for my ceremony. He attended my graduation, although most of my family had no clue that he was there for me. My sister and brother-in-law knew because he was a previous neighbor, but they didn't see any reason to intrude into my personal life. None of my family did at that point because I was legally grown.

With all I had experienced, there wasn't much anyone could tell me, and they knew it. Those two years of my life molded me into the strong woman I had become. With every trial and every experience, I gained strength. After all that I had endured, my resilience prevailed.

Part III

*D*uring my senior year of high school, I moved in with my other sister, which was my first time living in a household without my mother and Fanny. I continued working to financially support myself, as I had been doing since 16 years old. Still hurting from my ex-boyfriend and scared of trusting another man, I entered situationships with different men at the same time. I never held back in letting these men know that they couldn't be in a real relationship with me, but I enjoyed being a tease. They assumed sex would follow our dates, but 99% of the time, they were left disappointed. Once they realized I wouldn't offer my body in exchange for something less valuable, we stopped talking or I'd eventually cut them off. Even with the unhealed wounds of growing up without my father's presence, I honestly thought too highly of myself to give my body away to just any man. None of these men had earned my heart or the honor of being intimate with me, although I did give my body up a few times, resulting in unhealthy soul ties.

As an 18 year-old woman, I yearned for the attention of older men, since I didn't have many memories of spending much time with my father. His idea of quality time meant picking Fanny and I up from "home", taking us to the corner store, and riding around the hood before dropping us off at one of our family members' homes. He wouldn't come pick us up until the next day. I never developed a strong bond with my father. As a result, my life was void of the masculine affection I wanted and needed. My daddy issues negatively affected every relationship I had with another man. I was hurting from my father's lack of presence, effort, and support in my life, so I distracted my pain with the presence of random men.

But in spite of my pain, I was still focused on my future so I started applying for college scholarships to escape my current circumstances. One evening, as I slept on the floor of my young nephew's bedroom, my hard work finally paid off. I received an email for a $16,000 scholarship! Initially, the directors had rejected my application but after a second review, they invited me to an interview. Thankfully, I did well, and was blessed with an amazing scholarship award. The first people I shared my exciting news with were my college prep program mentors, as they were the ones who had encouraged me to complete the application in the first place. They had also pushed me to complete my college applications, even when I wanted to hang out with friends and boys. As a result, I was accepted into a university in Southern California! Now that my finances for college were figured out, I was ready to begin this next phase of my life.

The summer before leaving for college, I moved in with my older brother. What a relief! My brother willingly opened his doors to me, providing my very own room and bathroom, without charge. This was no surprise. When my brother moved back to our home state, he immediately began financially contributing to our family, although he lived on his own. He had helped my mom pay rent, assisted with our extracurricular activities, and even paid for special events like proms. In a way, my brother stood in the gaps of where my father lacked. My brother has and will always be one of the most important men in my life, as he was the first example I had as to what a genuine, Godly man looked like during my late teenage years. This particular summer, I also met a new guy friend who I continued to talk to for the next six years.

Reflections

*H*ow would you describe your male relationships throughout your life? Think about your male family members. Did your father, brothers, uncles and grandfathers protect, nurture, affirm, and/or provide for you in the ways you needed to be? Or were you subjected to abuse or neglect by them? Did you have any voids that you allowed the wrong men to fill, resulting in unhealthy bonds, attachments known or soul ties?

Our early encounters with boys and men, whether positive or negative, can determine the type of romantic relationships we engage in. This isn't always the case, but many young girls without the example of a strong male figure, preferably a father, tend to get into unhealthy relationships as they become teenagers and adults. It's hard to blame them - girls and women alike dream of falling in love one day. We yearn for love and to be loved. Yet, when you've never truly experienced the consistent presence of a high-quality man, it can become difficult to attract one. As a result, many women allow the wrong men to stay in their lives for too long. Nevertheless, we must focus on loving ourselves and healing from any hurt caused by men in our lives.

It's important to forgive every man who did you wrong in the past. Maybe those men had unaddressed issues of their own and unfortunately, you had to suffer because of it. There's no excuse for why he wasn't there or why he did you wrong. It wasn't your fault that you got hurt. However, it is your responsibility to take necessary steps to forgive and heal. It's wise to take the initiative in discovering and healing your heart from all unhealthy soul ties. Each of our healing processes will look different, but whatever action you decide, take full ownership in moving forward. What that man did, either purposely or unknowingly, could have ruined your life. But instead, you're growing from it. Don't allow him to prevent you from experiencing the healthy love you desire and deserve. Forgive him and move on with your life. Sis, heal.

CHAPTER 3

Risky Decisions

Part I

After graduating high school, the one and only thing that grasped my attention was the desire to make money as fast as my sugar daddy did, every day hustling. He was reluctant to show me the game in the beginning of our situationship. Eventually, as time passed, I finessed him into believing that he could trust me by showing him loyalty. Finally, his guard was down, and he was ready to teach me the game. Over the next year, our time was spent making money almost every weekday. We'd utilize the weekends to go out and have a good time. We attended social events, concerts, clubs, fancy restaurants - anywhere I wanted to go, we went. I was no longer embarrassed to be seen in public with him because I wasn't concerned with what others thought. He had elevated my life to a new level with the game he taught me and the finer lifestyle he exposed me to. For me, that was all that mattered.

Eventually, I became bored with sitting back while I watched him do all the work to bring in the money. Eager to get my hands dirty, he put me in position to hustle on my own. I was making more money than I had ever seen in my life which was the reason I quit working at McDonalds. With more free time available, I decided to enroll in the nearest community college. I always had a passion for learning and was ready to focus on school again. When I wasn't at school or studying, we hustled everyday like it was a 9-5 job. At the end of the day, we'd go to our hotel room, count all the money that was made, and he'd tell me to take what I wanted. At that point, I became fed up with living out of hotel rooms, and was determined to get my first apartment. I started saving all the money I was making and before I knew it, I had saved almost $10,000 in less than a month. This was the beginning of a new emotion I had never experienced before - greed.

That same emotion was the reason I caught my first case. I was arrested and escorted by 2 police officers to their patrol car. So many thoughts were running through my mind as I was being transported in the back of a police car to jail, feeling disappointed in myself. Luckily, I didn't have to sit in jail for long because he was there ready to bail me out when I called. After being released, I vowed to never go back. Not less than a week later, I was back in jail. The police had been doing an investigation which resulted in a warrant being issued out for my arrest. Completely unaware, I was on my way to school before being pulled over by the police. I was ordered to get out of my vehicle; they took my phone, money, and towed my car along with all my belongings in the trunk. With a bond of $350,000, and no way to get out, I spent 72 hours waiting to be officially charged with crimes they were investigating. Thankfully, no charges were filed at that moment and I was released from jail, again. Soon enough, I was back there days later. When I went to the police station to pick up my property, I was reprimanded immediately; they had officially filed criminal charges against me. By this time, I was exhausted and traumatized from being arrested 3 times in less than 2 weeks.

I sat in jail for almost 2 weeks while I waited to go to court for sentencing. In court, I watched the look of disappointment on my mother's face as the judge read my charges and sentenced me to 45 days in jail with 2 years' court probation. I couldn't tell if she was more disappointed in my unlawful actions or her lack of proper parenting that possibly contributed to the downward spiral of my life. Either way, she and I were relieved after I was released later that evening with time served and an order from the judge to do community service.

After all I had experienced, I was sick of the life I was living in California. I had gotten dismissed from school due to missing too many classes. I was tired of the sexual slave I had become to my sugar daddy. As much as I enjoyed making money, I was fed up with all the things that came with the lifestyle. I had became caught up in the moment with him, I failed to recognize the negative mental effect I allowed him to have over my life. The only person I wanted and needed at the moment was my first love.

We had only connected a few times since the abortion of our unborn seed. Last I heard from him, he was in a relationship and I was under the impression they were still living together, happily. I was unaware they had separated and he was dealing with his own harsh battles at the same time I was. Our commonality of pain seemed to had drawn us back together. As we reconnected, it became evident to him that I no longer was the innocent little girl he grew up with all those years. Although I was cautious of not exposing the raunchy lifestyle I lived without him, I didn't hesitate to show him how I was making money. I exposed the game to him, which marked the beginning of a new life for us together. I hadn't completely left my sugar daddy but he was no longer a main priority to me. My first love was back to give the only love I'd ever wanted, besides my father's love.

When he suggested that I move to Texas with him, I didn't hesitate to accept his offer. This time, I was an adult and there was no one that could stop me from living my life the way I wanted. We were finally back together and trying to have our first child. After a few weeks, things started to shift within our atmosphere. We were constantly fighting and arguing, which resulted in me leaving Texas, and moving back to California. With nowhere to go, I reached back out to the one person that I knew would accept me - my sugar daddy. He didn't notice I was pregnant because I wasn't showing at all. I decided that I was going to finish my prenatal care in California and figure out the dynamics of my relationship with my first love, later.

Nothing could have prepared me for what I was about to experience at my first doctor's visit in California. I was 11 weeks pregnant when the doctors searched anxiously for the heartbeat of my unborn child; they didn't find it. When they shared the news, I couldn't help but curl up in fetal position and cry. I felt so empty inside knowing I was carrying a dead fetus. After I called my first love with the news, I heard the pain in his voice. I was disappointed that I couldn't give him what he wanted. With no place of my own, I went back to my sister's house that my mom and I were staying in.

Hours after leaving my doctor's appointment, I began to bleed heavily. I got in the shower and after a few minutes, I started screaming for my mother as I watched the placenta covered in blood fall from in between my legs into the tub. Never having witnessed anything like that before, I was traumatized with fear. I couldn't bear the sight of seeing my unborn seed lying at the drain of the tub. My mother rushed into the bathroom and without hesitation, picked up my miscarried child with her bare hands. She quickly wrapped it in a paper towel and put it to the side while she tried to console me. After a few minutes, I began to calm down, but I was still in severe pain and bleeding excessively. My mother frantically called the ambulance while she watched me hemorrhage over the towels she had placed on the living room floor for me to lie down on. The ambulance was there within minutes and immediately began trying to stop the bleeding.

I miscarried on April 2, 2012, a day I'll never forget. I called my first love to update him on all that happened; he didn't hesitate to catch the next flight out to be by my side. By the time I had gotten to the hospital, I lost a tremendous amount of blood. I had to get an emergency blood transfusion after receiving a D&C. I didn't understand why all of this was happening to me, but I felt comforted with my first love and my mother by my side. This situation allowed us to put aside our differences, so I moved back to Texas with him and within a couple of days, we were signing the lease to our new townhome together.

However, we were incapable of creating a healthy relationship. Over the course of the next 6 months, I left and came back 4 more times. Every time I'd leave, I found myself back into the presence of my sugar daddy, although that wasn't quite where I wanted to be. I was addicted to the emotional dependence of my toxic male companions. I assumed the connection with my first love was based on true love and was the reason I couldn't leave him for good; in fact, the toxic soul ties I had created with him and every other man of my past hindered my ability to be alone. Every time I attempted to leave, we fought or argued, as he expressed his hurt in rage by throwing all of my belongings outside in the dirt. Other times, he would try to keep all the money we had saved together, leaving me with nothing. I became addicted to the pain in my relationship and leaving no longer became an option. Since I had gotten used to having my own place, I settled, refusing to go back to being unstable, living in hotel rooms.

As my relationship continued to remain toxic, I began focusing more on myself. Feeling like time was passing me by, I enrolled in a two-year college to reignite my passion for learning and my dreams of attending a four-year university like my sister, Vickey. I had no idea what I wanted to major in - I just knew school gave me a sense of the productivity I lacked. I was going to school a few days out of the week and hustling on the days I didn't have class. Between my hustle and his, we were bringing in more money than I had ever seen in my life. During that time, we didn't put as much effort into saving money as we did into spending it. We splurged on custom jewelry, Rolex watches, and designer handbags. We also went on expensive trips around the country to places like New York and Puerto Rico, staying at the most luxurious hotels and dining at the finest restaurants. Young, flashy, and admired by our peers, we were what most considered "hood rich." As my desire to maintain a flashy lifestyle increased, my desire to remain in school diminished. I eventually stopped going, even though I had taken out almost $10,000 dollars in student loans.

I began to realize just how different our lives had become during our three years apart. While I was out in the world lost, my first love had transformed into a man I was never fully exposed to until after we reconnected. He had acquired his own businesses before turning 18: an ice cream truck, a barbecue trailer, and a barbershop. A part of me felt envious towards him because his life seemed to have been going well while we were separated. It was the complete opposite from what I had experienced. By the time we were back together, he only had the ice cream truck. Still mentally invested into being the entrepreneur he was destined to be, but discouraged by the temporary setbacks, his focus on business slowly began to shift.

Traumatized from the miscarriage I had experienced the year before, I remained very cautious from the beginning when I discovered I was pregnant again. I was excited to know we were finally about to have our baby! Suddenly, our worlds came crashing down, again. Unexpectedly, I experienced my second consecutive miscarriage. I experienced a level of severe depression which no one was able to help me through. I was starting to believe I would never be able to conceive. However, I didn't spend a lot of time grieving over the miscarriage, as I tried to suppress my disappointment with the lavish lifestyle I had created for myself. Experiencing losses was the one thing that brought us closer together, no matter what we were going through in our relationship. Although I didn't know it at the moment, those miscarriages made me realize how God delayed my blessings since I was not ready to receive them.

We eventually became bored with the environment we were surrounded by in Texas, and were ready for a change. We decided to move to Georgia to experience something new. To our surprise, we were expecting again. Scarred from my past experiences, we kept the excitement to a minimum until I was in my third trimester. We had no family or friends in Georgia, and were dealing with unpleasant experiences, which resulted in us moving after only 6 months. Reluctant to move to Texas again, we decided to move back to our hometown in California. The constant moving seemed normal to me, due to the instability of my childhood.

At 7 months pregnant, I was on the road with my son driving a U-Haul truck from Georgia to California. We made it in less than 36 hours and were ready to begin searching for our place as soon as we arrived. By this time, our relationship was in complete turmoil due to my hormonal changes. We became more distant as he avoided confrontation with me by coming home late or sometimes, not at all. As his cheating intensified, so did my urge to invade his privacy, which ultimately led to fights. Sometimes, I was the aggressor because I felt like I had lost control of my relationship. I failed to realize that nothing I said or did was going to change him.

During my pregnancy, I experienced a deep depression like never before. I promised myself to never get pregnant again. I found it hard to cope with the lack of feeling loved or wanted by the man I thought loved me; as a result, I stopped caring about my physical appearance. He left me feeling emotionally and physically abandoned during what was supposed to be the most precious times of our lives. I was heartbroken. As time passed, he eventually started to build a relationship with a woman who he claimed was his cousin, at the time. My intuition said otherwise; I knew his friendship with the other woman was deeper than what he presented it to be. The same woman would eventually become one to furthermore contribute to the lust, chaos and ultimate demise of our relationship.

Part II

*A*fter a short, seven-hour drive filled with hugs and tears, my mother, youngest brother, and sister-in-law dropped me off at the University of California, Riverside. While most families walked their new college freshmen up to the dorm room, I walked back to mine alone. I stood in the middle of the room, staring at three beds and a small closet. The room was barely big enough for one person but the thought of sharing this room with two strangers brought tears to my eyes. I felt alone already, as I knew I wouldn't be able to depend on my family for support. I didn't know what type of experience was ahead of me but I had already decided I was in control of my future, through God's guidance. I refused to ever be poor or homeless again.

For the most part, I enjoyed college life. I met good friends, joined different organizations, and partied almost every weekend, while continuing to achieve good grades. I seized the new opportunities of my environment, allowing myself to welcome growth in every way possible. I no longer identified with the hurt girl from my past, as I was now on my journey towards becoming the woman God called me to be. Or maybe, I had been on this journey all along. I decided to major in Business Administration with a concentration in Management. I became intrigued with the thought of one day running my own business, although I had never personally known an entrepreneur. I started working for the university as a program associate, where I was in charge of planning, promoting, and eventually managing different events like art shows, game nights, and music festivals. Whether at work or in the classroom, I always found myself leading my peers or projects. Looking back over my life, I realized I was born to lead, as I held many leadership positions throughout my youth. Now in college, I was able to realize and tap into my natural, God-given gift of leadership.

Near the end of my junior year, I was accepted into a paid leadership development program to become a retail manager. I interned with this company throughout my senior year of college, while also balancing my university job and school work. Upon graduation, I was offered a full-time position as an assistant store manager. Unaware of the dreadful working environment of retail, I accepted the position and stopped applying myself towards other career opportunities. As a 22 year old recent college graduate, I was making more money than most of my family members and peers. My salary was high enough for me to live comfortably, but I still felt uneasy. Instead of focusing on building a solid foundation for my life, I fed into my discontent from working in retail. I eventually requested to be relocated back near my hometown, as I knew I would not be at this job long. I moved into a nice apartment, two cities away from where my family lived. Eventually, I applied for a position with a top retail bank and landed a great position as an operations manager. I loved working at the bank, as it aligned better with my business degree. My work schedule, benefits, and salary weren't bad at all. I could see myself growing with this company over the next few years; however, just 3 months into my new position, I started growing unsatisfied again. I remember going outside to call my mom during break and I broke down crying. I didn't understand why I was so uncomfortable there. My co-workers were fun. My job duties weren't the worse. I enjoyed my work-life balance. Were these jobs the actual problem or was it just me? Why couldn't I remain settled in one place for a long period of time? It was clear that my past still had an effect on my life. Even though I was living comfortably on my own, without struggling financially, I couldn't find stability. Moving from place to place had become a normal lifestyle during my youth and teenage years; now as an adult, living a structured lifestyle was foreign, so I ran every time it was presented to me.

Feeling extremely unfulfilled, I began to read self-help books and attend different seminars. I also hired a life coach. Instantly, my desire to discover my purpose was ignited. Right away, I made the decision to no longer live an average, routine life. I now desired to build a life that I loved. At 23 years old, I promised myself I would begin striving towards excellence in all areas of my life, including financially, spiritually, mentally, emotionally, and physically. I had a plan for improving every area and began to execute immediately.

Spiritually, I was already working towards improving my relationship with God and feeding my mind. I had joined an amazing church during my junior year of college and even got baptized. Now, I planned to be more intentional about my Christian walk and chose to give up habits I had formed, such as smoking weed, drinking excessively, and having premarital sex. The strengthening of my relationship with God marked the beginning of my healing journey.

Emotionally, I was ready to end a situationship with the second man I ever felt loved by. He was one of the men I met while staying with my brother, the summer before leaving for college. We talked for about an hour; then, a few weeks later, I left for college. I assumed we would never see or speak to each other again, but during my first year in college, he consistently communicated with me. Once I came home during summer break, we began to see each other weekly. Over time, he expressed his love for me. Eventually, I felt the same, as I began to develop a deep, strong lust, mistaken as love, for him. He was always so gentle, affectionate, and present. I had never experienced this from a man before, so I became addicted to him although he never truly valued me. We spent time together, yet he rarely took me on dates. We were with each other during special holidays, but he never bought me gifts. We weren't in a relationship since he didn't meet my standards at all except for looks, yet still, I continued to see him and give him sexual benefits without a real commitment. I tried to change him. He was a few years older than me, but could never maintain a stable job, a place to stay, or a car. He was a drug user and stole from those around him, including me. He also had other women. I wanted his love and commitment, which was something he could not give to me. Now realizing my worth, I was ready to move on from him.

Financially, I created a plan to reduce my monthly rent by 75%, allowing more money for savings, debt payments, and investments. I decided to move out of my own apartment and back into my brother's home for about 6 months, as we realized we could both help each other reach our financial goals. Instead of paying $2,000 on rent and household bills, I was now paying my brother only $550 per month. I put the extra money towards the small personal loans and credit card debt I had accumulated over the years. Eventually, the only debt I owed were student and car loans. I decided that living in California was too expensive for my $60,000 annual income. Within the next few weeks, I began making plans toward moving to a new state I had never been to before and didn't know anyone in. I sold my car for the exact amount I owed and paid it off, which meant student loans were the only debt left to pay. I donated most of my furniture and clothing. At work, I put in the relocation request with my market manager. He approved it. I was all set to move across the country. My family didn't think it was a good decision, as I currently had a nice bank job and comfortable lifestyle. I had been making my own decisions since teenage years, so while I appreciated their concerns, my mind was already made up. Once the last day at my job arrived, relocating started to become a reality.

During this time, I also received an internal recommendation to work as a manager's assistant for one of the top consulting firms in the world. I had never shared my desires to work there with anyone but this was a dream company to me! I had some big decisions to make. Should I stay in the Bay Area, where the job market was amazing, or bet on myself towards thriving in an unknown place? Less than a week after receiving the email requesting my resume for the consulting firm position, I boarded my flight to Atlanta, Georgia. I chose to venture off into an unknown place, which also meant the official end of my six-year toxic situationship. A few days before my departure, I saw him one last time. Right before I drove off, I looked him right in the eyes and told him he would never see me again. I kept my word. Now, I was ready to begin the next phase of my journey.

On Independence Day, I arrived in Atlanta with three or four suitcases. Once there, I went to my Airbnb, as I planned on staying there until I could secure an apartment. I found a house to rent a room in, but that living arrangement didn't even last a week since the home was infested with huge bugs I had never seen before. Welcome to the South! I bought a car and moved into my own apartment a week later. During this time, I was also focused on maintaining my full-time employment. I went to a few bank branches to see if there were any positions available. I eventually landed an interview with the market manager. After the interview, he connected with my program manager and things did not go well from there. There had been a communication disconnect between all the managers I reported to. She had no idea I had moved to Atlanta. My immediate manager had approved my relocation but out of nowhere, he resigned, possibly because of health reasons. My interim manager was informed about my move, but she told my program manager she didn't know I had moved already. After speaking with a few decision-makers, my program manager told me I had 30 days to find another position within the bank, or I would have to resign. I eventually resigned, as I couldn't find a position. I was not worried at the time, as I thought I had enough money to last for the next few months. However, since I ate out regularly and attended different events, I eventually drained my savings account and eventually my 401K. I couldn't find another job opportunity that paid enough, so I decided to join the side gig community. I was on my grind, sometimes bringing in hundreds of dollars on the weekends, which meant more in Georgia than it would have in California. Side work sustained me for a few months but near the end of the year, I began to struggle a little financially. I remember one month, for the first time ever, I was going to be short on my rent. On the 1st of the month, I went to my online rent portal and shockingly, it said I only owed half the amount of my full rent. Praise God! A few weeks prior, I had emailed corporate about a bug issue I was having in my apartment. They never responded back but it's possible this was their way of accommodating the inconvenience. Overall, I knew this was a sign from God, knowing He would always take care of me. It didn't matter if I didn't have any family or close friends in Atlanta, as long as I had a relationship with Him, I'd always be well taken care of.

As the year came to an end and I reflected on my decision to move, I became excited about my future. Most importantly, I was happy with my willingness to take such a huge risk. I knew the risk would lead to a greater reward.

Reflection

*W*hat's the biggest risk you've ever taken? Reflect over your life. Are you currently living a comfortable, predictable life? Or have you created one filled with surprises and challenges along the way? We all have different purposes and focuses in life so one lifestyle, whether risky or not, shouldn't be viewed as better than the other. Each person will experience different levels of victories and tribulations along the way. Just remember, we will only experience one life here on

Earth. It's never too late to make the moves you've always talked about but never got around to.

Even if you've made terrible, risky decisions that have cost you to lose money, time, relationships, or even your freedom, it's time to forgive yourself for what you did or did not do.

You are not your mistakes, move on. As long as you're still breathing, there's still time to improve the quality of your life. Reflect on the past, but don't stay there too long. Instead, focus on your present and plan for the future. No decision or risk is too big for you to bounce back from. Sis, Heal.

CHAPTER 4

Toxic vs Real Love

Part I

I fought hard to keep my family together, despite knowing I'd have to stay in a toxic relationship.

I didn't want my son being raised in dysfunction, growing up in two separate homes. I did what so many women have done - sacrificed happiness to keep the family together. I remained faithful in spite of him not reciprocating that same quality. I assumed he would eventually see my value if I served and pleased him more.

After feeling unappreciated for so long, I recognized my emotions toward him began to change. He was temporarily crippled after being shot in his ankle on New Year's Eve, less than 2 weeks before our son was due. I couldn't find the love in my heart to be as compassionate as I wanted to be towards him. I was thankful he was alive, but I was suffering deeply from feeling emotionally abandoned during the most precious time in my life. So, in return, I wanted him to feel the same. Struggling to control my emotions, my love was turning into pure hate and resentment.

The day finally came for my son to make his grand entrance into the world. There was nothing that could take away the joy he and I shared, watching the birth of our child. For the first time in my life, I felt a love I had never experienced before. At that moment, I vowed to give my son a life I never had growing up. I looked into my child's father's eyes as he thanked me for giving him the biggest blessing he'd ever receive. I could tell the feeling we shared for our son was mutual - unconditional love.

Regardless of our relationship issues, I couldn't discredit the loving present father I watched him become. I appreciated the effort he put forth into being a father and family man every day after our son was born. I was exposed to a vulnerable yet protective side of him I had never seen before. When he walked, he moved with a newfound purpose in life. My love for him grew based on the role he played in our son's life, along with his ability to stay committed to handling his responsibilities. At that moment, I knew that he'd always be present to live and die for my son and me, his family.

I was in love with being a mother and had shifted all of my focus on nurturing my son. Wanting the very best for my firstborn from the beginning, I spent the first 6 months of his life breastfeeding him. He quickly became accustomed to feeding on my breast and refused to take the bottle, which required me to practically be a full-time mother. It was exhausting yet fulfilling. While I stayed home with our son, my child's father made sure we were good, financially. I appreciated his willingness to be the only provider for us during and after my pregnancy. After deciding that California wasn't a desirable place for us to raise our son, we moved back to Texas. Soon after getting settled into our townhome, it didn't take long for me to become pregnant again. It was evident that I was a fertile woman, just like my mother. Although we didn't have plans on bringing another child into the world so soon, an abortion ultimately wasn't an option for us.

He was back. Unfortunately, unexpected trouble resulted in him going to jail for 6 months while I raised our son on my own, pregnant. I didn't want to be taken out of my son's life, so I decided to switch my moves up. I applied for a job at Macy's and got hired almost immediately. Dissatisfied and feeling like I was too good to work there, I decided to apply for a job at the bank. I was hired within 2 weeks, but due to my failed background check, I was fired on my first day. Feeling discouraged, I went back to what I knew, hustling. Things weren't hard for me while he was in jail because I was a woman that knew how to hold it down. I took the responsibility of now being the temporary head of my household and provider for my family. My life had revolved around being a mother and a supportive girlfriend, which left me with little time to focus on myself. I supported him 100% while he was in jail, visiting him frequently while remaining loyal, honest, and faithful. After getting into more trouble while locked up, he was faced with new charges. When his release date approached, he was given a bond and released. We were reunited and loving on each other as if nothing else mattered. I cherished that moment because I felt genuinely wanted and needed by him. Still, with a case pending, our moment of celebration couldn't last long as I was facing the potential of being a single mother again if he had to go back to jail.

Before we knew it, the day came for our daughter to make her grand entrance into the world. If I had to choose one word to describe that day, it was bittersweet. The same day our daughter was scheduled to be born was the same day I discovered I'd be a single mother of 2 for 11 months. He was still in court when I began going into labor while home alone. His dad rushed over to my house to pick me up and transport me to his house. After hours of unbearable pain with contractions less than 5 minutes apart, his dad rushed me to the nearest hospital. The nurses checked my cervix immediately upon arrival. I was 7 centimeters dilated and was denied an epidural. Worried that my children's father would miss the birth of our daughter, I pleaded for the nurses to call him as they transported me to delivery.

I was 8 centimeters when I made it into the delivery room but with my legs down, I refused to push until the nurses rushed him into the room seconds later. My precious baby girl was delivered after only a few pushes and I immediately fell in love with her. As I held my firstborn daughter, I looked into her innocent eyes as I promised to not repeat the same mistakes from my past. I knew we'd need the extra support so their grandmother flew from California to Texas to assist us with the kids. With all of my family and the majority of his living in California, we made the decision to move back while he served his sentence in Texas. Five days after my daughter was born, we packed up everything and drove from Texas to California in a U-Haul truck. My son flew back to California with his grandmother. We made it to California in under 24 hours and immediately began searching for an apartment.

Less than one month after my daughter was born, we were back on the road on our way out of town to make money. Hustling was one thing we did well together. Everything had been going smooth until we had an unexpected interaction with the police. I frantically made a bad decision after we were being pulled over in a retail parking lot. I was nervous when we were both summoned to get out of the car. After a few minutes of being patted down by the police, I was allowed to get back into the car. He, on the other hand, was arrested for a petty crime which resulted in him having to spend a few hours in jail before I was able to bail him out. A bit shook up, we ended the trip early and caught the next flight out in the morning. We had no idea that we'd eventually endure the consequences of that trip years later.

We were back in California, getting prepared for him to fly back to Texas to serve time in prison. With so much going on,

I had no idea about the plans he had set for us in the upcoming days. We went to the mall and he purchased me a white and pink floral designed Roberto Cavalli dress with a pair of white Christian Louboutin heels. I spent the rest of the day, upon his request, prepping for a special day he'd planned. The next day, we got into our BMW 750i and he blindfolded me as we drove from his mother's house to an unknown destination. By this time, I had butterflies in my stomach as I wondered where had we arrived in less than 5 minutes. Still blindfolded, he assisted me out of the car and we walked until we reached a grassy area. After a few seconds, he pulled off my blindfold, and I gasped as I stood in the middle of the school's field where we met in 6th grade. A photographer stood close by, capturing every moment while we sat down at a small table decorated with chocolate-covered dessert, roses, and balloons. I stood speechless as he gazed into my eyes telling me how much he adored and appreciated me for the woman I was to him.

After we sat down, I tried to gather my thoughts to find the words to express how amazing I felt, but I couldn't. After a few moments, his sister and my niece walked out onto the field dressed in butler attire as they served us fresh champagne and hors d'oeuvres. Then, there was a guy walking towards us holding what looked like a dozen doves in a small cage. My children's father came over to my side, assisted me out of my chair, and we watched as doves were released into the sky. When I turned around, there he was kneeling on one knee, holding a ring flushed with diamonds asking me to marry him. My eyes filled with tears as I looked into his eyes with total satisfaction. I grabbed his face and kissed him uncontrollably, crying, and saying yes repeatedly. Moments later, our families appeared out of nowhere running onto the field ready to embrace me as I cried tears of joy. Soon after, a violinist came onto the field to play some of our favorite R&B love songs. That night was like nothing I had ever experienced before and something I had only seen in a movie. At that moment, it felt like I had fallen in love with him all over again.

Unfortunately, the day came for him to go to court to be officially sentenced and reprimanded. Although I was disappointed that my family would have to be separated again, I did my best to maintain my strength. My kid's father risked his freedom for the sake of our well-being, and I appreciated him for it. When it was time for him to approach the stand to be sentenced and taken into custody, I fought to hold back my tears. The judge read his sentencing and he was taken into custody seconds later. He turned around and we simultaneously mouthed "I love you" as he was escorted away in handcuffs. I left the courtroom immediately after, crying yet relieved that it was finally over.

The following months for me were filled with being a full-time mother while I hustled to maintain the lifestyle we were accustomed to. Although I no longer wanted to risk my freedom for a living, I knew that getting a job wouldn't cover all of my living expenses along with the cost of supporting my fiancé. I was flying from California to Texas frequently, sometimes with both of our children just to get a 4-hour visit with him. During his 11-month stay in prison, we talked almost every day. I wrote him letters frequently, sent him pictures, books, and magazines. Once again, I showed him that I was loyal to him through thick and thin.

As the time approached for him to be released from jail, I did everything I could to prepare. Deciding to move once again, I flew back to Texas. After applying for a house and getting approved, I immediately begin to pack. I picked up a U-Haul truck, scheduled moving assistance, and picked up workers who were standing in the Home Depot parking lot. After everything was packed up and moved out, I noticed my engagement ring had been stolen. It was so big that I had to take it off to remove my TV from off the wall; that was the last time I saw it. I was devastated because it was stolen before I could insure it. I cried for hours as I waited to tell my fiancé about the incident.

Eventually, the day finally came for him to be released and I couldn't hide my excitement. I patiently waited in the line of cars as the guard approached each vehicle retrieving our information for us to enter the building. A few minutes later, my fiancé emerged from the prison doors wearing Balenciaga sneakers and a Balmain sweatsuit I purchased him. He embraced us with hugs and kisses as I became overwhelmed with emotions seeing my family being reunited again. We spent the next few weeks enjoying our family and our home. He kept expressing how proud he was of me for all that I had accomplished. Everything was perfect.

As my fiancé's birthday approached, we agreed that we both deserved to take a trip to Florida together. In preparation for our upcoming trip, we decided to take a trip to make money for the first time since he had been released. We flew to California, dropped our children off, and were flying out to a different state a few days later. Two days into the trip, we had made more money in one day then we'd ever had before. Feeling uneasy, we left the state we were in and flew to the next one. Ignoring all the red flags, we went to our hotel and prepped for "work" the next day.

After arguing all morning, our vibe for the day was interrupted as we were distracted throughout the day. Due to a small dispute with employees inside of a building, we were pulled over by the police and suspiciously questioned. After a few moments, I was ordered out of the driver's side of the vehicle and arrested immediately. Soon after, I watched as my fiancé was escorted from the car and placed in handcuffs as well. We were both taken to the police station, and the car with all of our belongings was towed. I was placed in an interrogation room while he was outside the door with the officers; under no circumstances were we going to snitch on each other. Eventually, my fiancé was taken to jail, and I followed shortly after. Only in jail for a minor charge, I was released on a small bond later that evening. My fiancé was being held on a no-bail hold, and there was nothing that I could do about it. Scared to go up to the police station to retrieve our items, in fear of being arrested again, I decided to leave the state with my fiancé's consent and go back to California to pick up our children.

The next few weeks felt like a complete nightmare to me. My fiancé was in jail, and I couldn't access the money we had without him being present. I was too scared to hustle, but I knew I had to do what needed to be done. When the day finally came for him to be granted a bail, I didn't hesitate to pay the necessary fees for him to be released. He eventually flew back home the next day to be reunited with my children and I. When it was time for him to go to court in the state we were both arrested in, I went with him. I also went to the police station to pick up our items and had no idea that I would be arrested when I arrived. I was charged with the same crime he had been charged with. I remained calm as I sat in jail, helplessly waiting for my fiancé to bond me out, and sure enough, I was released later that day.

We flew back home and after that incident, everything seemed to be falling apart and coming together at the same time. With so much stress brewing in the both of us from the thought of leaving our kids, we were constantly fighting and arguing. Under more pressure than what we seemingly could handle, we were not mature enough to be the support system that we both needed.

Due to the decisions I made, I was facing the potential of spending years of incarceration and being away from my kids. I was caught up in trying to provide the best life for them, but of course, that lifestyle had consequences. Apart of me felt like I was repeating the cycle of my mother's habits. Hustling became an addiction that I couldn't resist. I remained strong through it all, not allowing the situation to take a toll on me. My fiancé was facing the same consequences as I was, but his were much harsher due to his extensive criminal record. Exhausted with the consequences that hustling brought us, my fiancé was determined to rebirth his entrepreneurial spirit. Instead of becoming defeated, he used our negative situation to birth something positive.

Part II

began to network more frequently as I took my professional development seriously. During one event, I connected with the recruiter of a family fun entertainment center. They loved me and scheduled an interview right away with the general manager. A few days later, I received an invite to interview with the district manager. On the day of the interview, I completely showed out by asking for a salary that was similar to what I was making in California. I was in Georgia now, where the average market pay for that position was much lower than it would have been in California. Knowing this, I left the interview that day not planning on hearing back from them, as my salary requirements were above what they were willing to pay me. Surprisingly, I received an offer letter for an assistant manager position in my email. The pay was still too low so I declined.

They countered my letter with a higher salary offer. Overall, the final pay wasn't bad at all, just lower than what I wanted to make at the time. Since my apartment lease was ending soon, and the company provided traveling opportunities, I decided to accept the job. A few days after the New Year began, I was off to Boston to train for my new position. Living in Massachusetts, about an hour away from Boston, was pretty interesting. From the snow storms to the slow pace, I was happy when the time came for me to return back to Georgia though. I quickly found another apartment to live in.

On my first day at my new job, I walked in as if I owned the place. Seriously. I wore a power-blue suit and heels. All my coworkers and even my general manager had on regular clothes. I didn't get the memo on what to wear for the first day so when it doubt, I always dressed to impress. Coincidentally, the district manager was there, and luckily, I was prepared for our first encounter. Later on, I went home to change into regular clothes since we would be getting dirty for the next few weeks, in preparation for the opening of our new store. Earlier on, my district manager expressed his plans of promoting me to my general manager.

On our job site, there were a lot of male contractors handling the construction of our building. As I headed to lunch one day, I jokingly told Fanny on the phone how I felt my husband was in the building. A few days later, a young and handsome electrician approached me while I was working on one of our machines. We talked for about fifteen minutes or so and then went back to working. He told me he was 23 at the time (although he had actually turned 22 recently-he lied); I was 24. On my way to lunch, I bumped into him again, and he detoured his route to follow me. He asked for my number. I had never given my personal digits to any man at work since I was against mixing business with personal. As a contractor, I knew he wouldn't be there for long, so after giving it a few seconds of thought, I gave him my number. The age difference didn't bother me since my life coach had suggested for me to consider dating younger men. He texted me over the next few days. On Valentine's Day morning, he asked to take me out. Funny thing is, I knew he would ask since he had been consistently texting me every day. I didn't respond until hours later; we decided to go eat near my home. We both loved Italian food, so he sent me the directions to Olive Garden! I politely declined and suggested the Steakhouse next door. During our date, I asked most of the questions to determine if he was worth my time. Although I had been on several dates over the last few months in my new city, I had become very guarded and careful of who I allowed into my life. I was at a point where I truly enjoyed my own company, and made myself happy. I was in the middle of rebuilding my career and just working on all areas of my life so I had no desire to be in a relationship. From what we talked about, I determined we could remain friends since he didn't meet my high standards. I also learned he was fresh out of a long-term relationship, so I refused to be his rebound. As we spent more time together, we instantly began to form a solid friendship. I invited him to celebrate my 25th birthday in Florida, and we drove down together. Strangely, I felt a deep sense of trust and peace with him. Although I had only known him for a little more than a month, I felt safe and protected. Our vacation was the beginning of a solid foundation and most importantly, he respected my decision to abstain from sex until marriage. Once we were back in Atlanta, he made his intentions of getting to know me very clear. He initiated daily communication and always took me on fun dates throughout the city. As he learned more about what I was looking for in a man, he slowly began to transform in all areas. He became a huge support system for me, as I lived so far away from family. We were still friends, but it became clear he wanted to be my man. I began to develop deep feelings for him, and I had no doubts he felt the same way.

Things were going well in my life but for some reason, I was ready to move again. Uh oh. The instability of my childhood was back. I loved living in Atlanta but since I was accustomed to moving around so much, I couldn't stay in one place for more than a year. When my director approached me with the possibility of being promoted to the general manager of my own store, I was beyond excited! I told him my top choices were either New York or back home to California. They sent me to New York for a few days to represent the company at a recruiting event for a new store location. Ultimately, they decided that San Jose, California would be my new home. This was such a divine opportunity, as my mother currently worked in that city. Over the last year, I had been praying that God would use me to help fix her housing situation, since she was still homeless.

By the end of the summer, I was all set to move back to California to manage my new store and provide a home for my mother. My guy friend hated the thought of me leaving only six months into our friendship, but he fully supported my decision to advance my career. This opportunity included an increase in my salary and a $1,700 monthly housing allowance. Yes, my job would be paying the majority of my rent every month. Although the cost of living in California was ridiculous, I decided I could make it work. During my last week in Atlanta, my guy friend and I spent every day together after we got off work. He made each date special and on our last day together, he surprised me with the most romantic zoo date, followed by a picnic at the lake. It was clear both of our feelings were strong for each other. We had been doing so well in our decision to abstain from sex but unfortunately, we slipped up that night. Admittedly, it was my idea. We never planned on beginning our courtship by fornicating, but we were certain we wanted to pursue God and marriage together. Neither of us had witnessed a heathy marriage up-close so we wanted to be the change agents for our families.

The next day, we officially began courting. I cried as my man dropped me off at the airport. I had grown to love him over the last 6 months. As we prepared to get out of the car, constant tears began to flow from his eyes. In that moment, I knew he loved me too. We sat there embracing each other, enjoying the last hugs and kisses we thought we would experience for a while. Eventually, I went off to board my flight to San Jose. Once landed, I went to my hotel. Within a week or two, I had found a two-bedroom apartment for me and my mother. It made me happy knowing my mother now had a place to call home.

Eventually, I flew back to Atlanta to see my man, on the company's dime. Before we departed this time, he said those three special words as he embraced me. It was amazing seeing his love for me, before he had ever said it. His actions, gentleness, and innocent affection had spoken volume over the last few months. But now, his love was confirmed through his words. Of course, I said it back. This moment was so special. I remember when I first met him, I promised I would be myself. Prior to him, I felt the need to act cold and uninterested towards men I met out of fear of being hurt. But this time was different. I allowed myself to be true to who I was and to trust him, letting go of the fear of being hurt again. Slowly, his love began to heal some wounds of my past. It was beautiful experiencing healthy love for the first time in my life.

Reflection

O ut of all the relationships you've been in, would you say that you've ever experienced healthy love? Or was the love you thought you shared with your man considered toxic? Real love embodies patience, kindness, care, thoughtfulness, forgiveness, and honesty, amongst many other things. Although no man is perfect, he should be striving to operate in real, healthy love. You deserve the kind of love that you can see with consistent actions; love is not lust and it is definitely not pain or any form of abuse. A toxic relationship, confused as love, will rob you of time, energy and resources you will never get back. You can't remain in an unhealthy relationship for too long. Yes, you may have thought it was real during the honeymoon phase but once you receive the red flags of a toxic or unhealthy relationship, you must leave sis. You aren't the first woman to make relationship judgement mistakes and you most certainly won't be the last. But, you must move on for yourself and the legacy you are creating. Your future life depends on the decisions you make today. Just know that real love will change your life for the better. You deserve to be loved properly. Sis, heal.

CHAPTER 5

New Beginnings

Part I

As a new general manager, I was performing very well. My team respected my leadership style but eventually, the usual retail headaches began to present itself. Just a few months into my promotion, I was fed up with getting off work at 3am two or three nights per week, being disrespected by customers, doing a portion of my manager's job while he got the credit for it, and listening to drama from department managers and my district manager. I knew I no longer wanted to be a part of this company, or any other retail work environment ever again. I left my last job and moved to Atlanta for a specific purpose so now, I was more determined than ever to complete my escape from working in retail for good.

My long-distance relationship continued to remain strong, as we traveled to see each other. Near the end of the year, we celebrated his 23rd birthday in Las Vegas. Once I returned back to work, my manager was relieved to see me. I called him into a private office and turned in my four-week' notice of resignation. The look on his face was priceless, as he knew he had contributed to the loss of a valuable team member. After five years of retail management, I had enough. I was ready to begin my entrepreneurship journey. I researched low-cost business ideas and decided to start a credit repair business as a Certified Credit Repair Consultant. My own credit was decent, but could use some work, so I practiced on myself. I had recently received an insurance settlement from a car accident, so I used the money to pay off my debt. I was back to only owing student loans and a car note. Over the next two months, I watched my credit score go up. My goal was to hit a score of 700. I passed that, easily. My next goal was 800. I hit a 797. I knew then, I was ready to start helping others, as I was now a credit repair expert. Although I now had a high credit score and minimal consumer debt, it was hard to keep up with my monthly expenses. Without the monthly rental allowance from my employer, I was paying close to $2500 in household rent and bills alone. My insurance settlement check didn't last long, although I was extremely proud of myself. Instead of using the money on fancy vacations or shopping trips, I paid off my debt and started a business. I also gave a portion away, as a strong believer of tithing. I had booked a few credit repair clients, but I wasn't producing enough income to cover monthly expenses. I started doing side gigs again but overall, I required more money to live on than what I was currently making. My mother was still living with me, rent-free, and wasn't able to help much, although she had a full-time job. The goal of moving her in was for her to save money for an apartment; but between her poor money habits and dealing with current financial challenges, the plan failed. I desired to move back to Atlanta right after I quit my job but my mother asked me to stay for a few more months; she had lost her sister and father back-to-back, so asked for my support. Staying meant I would be paying about $11,000 more to finish the remainder of my lease versus a $2,200 lease break fee. I wanted to continue to provide her with a place to stay for as long as I could, so I stayed for a few more months.

During the middle of the year, I made the move back to Atlanta. Shortly after my arrival, I moved into yet another apartment. I must admit, I did attempt to find another job but could not find a well-paying one. I was convinced that working a 9-5 job was not a part of my purpose, as I could not catch a break. From interview miscommunications to job offers being revoked and more, I became convinced that having a job was not the path God wanted me to be on during this season.

Instead of starting another job, I enrolled in real estate school with financial assistance from my Father - this was the first time I had ever asked anyone for help during my adult years. Less than two months later, I became a licensed Realtor. I had always planned on entering the real estate industry, as I frequently attended seminars and read books on the topic. I dreamed of becoming a real estate investor, so I viewed obtaining my license as a starting point. I joined a great brokerage company, and committed to fully learning how to successfully sell homes. Within 3 to 4 months, I sold my first home! I was officially working for myself. Initially, I had planned on having a full-time job while running my business, but since I still couldn't find one, I continued to dedicate all my efforts into real estate. Of course, starting a new business brought on financial and even emotional struggles and challenges I had never encountered before. As the months went by, entrepreneurship began to test and challenge literally every area of my life. Spiritually, I began to question whether God was still with me. Emotionally, I suffered from deep levels of depression and unhealthy thoughts. My relationships with friends, both new and old, began to suffer as well. Sadly, I had to end close, one-sided friendships that no longer served the direction my life was heading in. As the challenges increased, I thought of quitting, but always knew it wasn't an option. I had quit my last three positions when times became hard. This time, I allowed my current struggles to continue developing the characteristics and mindsets of the business woman God purposed me to be. At 27 years old, I refused to keep allowing the instability of my past to affect my future. By all means necessary, I would continue to press forward against obstacles and continue what I finished until my desired outcomes were reached. It was bigger than money; I was striving and believing towards a new breakthrough in my life. I knew this challenging season was preparing me for a greater lifestyle.

My strength of my relationship with my man was being tested, as well. He had been so supportive during all stages of my life, and this time was no different. He was used to seeing me as a strong, independent woman who had all her stuff together. As I became weaker in almost every area of my life, he poured into me in ways like never before. He constantly prayed over me during my moments of sorrow. He never failed to remind me of the strong woman I was and how we would overcome this season, together. He also helped me pay a few bills. Overall, he was still committed to my happiness, as he took me on vacations and our usual dates. We were still steadily moving towards our plans for the future and had always planned on waiting until that special day to move in together. However, since my lease was ending around the same time period he would be moving into his new apartment, we made the decision to live together. We talked about marriage often and from our conversations, I knew he would propose before the year was over, so I rationalized the decision of living together before marriage.

Part II

*I*n spite of all we were going through, my fiancé had placed all of his energy into creating a business for his family. After months of consistency and determination, we were officially business owners of a luxury transportation company. We purchased 2 buses and converted them into party buses. The moment became surreal when we had our first clients, one of the best American R&B groups of the late 1990's. Although I had never acquired my own business before, I immediately felt an undeniable drive towards achieving success. I was eager to get my hands dirty, ensuring that our business was ran properly. That moment birthed something in me that I never knew existed, an entrepreneurial spirit.

I stayed behind the scenes handling the administrative work for the business. I created our website, business cards, logo, and everything else we needed. As the weeks passed, we began focusing on how to build our clientele. Motivated to continue building legitimate income, my fiancé began utilizing his dealer's license to buy and sell cars. Eventually, I followed in his steps. I admired our ability to exert energy into something positive that we could finally be proud of. I was also proud of the start of a legacy we were creating for our children. I felt generational curses of poverty being broken, as our children watched us work diligently while running our business.

I was left to run our transportation business on my own after my fiancé was sentenced to jail. I felt the pressure of not wanting to disappoint my family, so I pushed harder to excel within our business. Incapable of handling all the positions alone, I hired an additional driver to assist me with the other vehicle. As our income became more consistent, I was proud of myself for sustaining what my fiancé had proudly created.

However, I still had to handle mistakes from my past. Since my court date was approaching, I flew my children to California to be with their grandmother while I served my time in jail. Eventually, the time came for me to go to court to face my fate. I was sentenced to 90 days in jail with the opportunity of serving time in a work release program. When the time came for my fiancé to be released, I was excited he was finally free, yet sad that I still had to serve time. He flew to California to pick up our children and take them back home to Texas.

I can't describe the feeling of when I was finally released from jail, to be reunited with my family. I embraced my children with tears swelling in my eyes, feeling like a failure. Although they didn't know I was in jail, I knew I would have to one day tell them the story. My mistakes were causing emotional scars just like my mother's and father's mistakes when I was a child. I was in fear of them growing up with a story to tell, that involved me leaving for days or weeks for the sake of money, just like my mother. At that moment, I vowed to be a better mother, no longer willing to sacrifice my freedom and taint my children's childhood memories.

With so much turmoil our relationship had endured, I was finally ready to walk away from the man I once imagined spending the rest of my life with. After months of living together with the idea of separating, I decided that it was time for my children's father to leave and get his own place. A month after he moved out, I was hit with an unexpected pregnancy again and was ultimately torn between the decision of what to do. I had experienced 2 abortions in between my recent children, and I didn't want to get another abortion. But I didn't think it was smart to bring another child into an unstable situation, so I decided to terminate the pregnancy.

Right before the day of my scheduled abortion, I had a disturbing dream. I became reluctant to continue on with the procedure and eventually changed my mind, continuing on with the pregnancy. Disappointed with myself for getting pregnant again, I hid the pregnancy from my family until I was 8 months. I didn't plan on telling my family until delivery but to my surprise, my sister Vickey paid me an unexpected visit so I could no longer hide it.

During those months, I couldn't help but feel resentment towards my child's father for his lack of support mentally, physically, and emotionally. Over time, expenses began to pile up quickly. Without much money coming in, I was almost broke and felt like I had no one to assist me during that time. While I assumed my fiancé was living a good life, I was struggling for the first time in my adulthood. In the beginning of our separation, we had spent time going back and forth with each other as we struggled from the toxic addictive soul tie we had formed over the years. There were moments when I genuinely didn't want to be with him and then, at times, I thought I wanted to make our relationship work. One evening, before his birthday, I was faced with the reality that no matter how much I loved him, he was never going to be the man that I wanted. I walked into his condo and wasn't surprised when I saw the same woman who contributed to the emotional trauma I had faced while pregnant with our first child, lying in his bed. Consumed with emotions of betrayal, I cried the whole way home. Although we weren't together, he knew the negative impact this woman had on our relationship years prior.

To ease my pain, I began focusing on the baby that I was getting ready to birth. As my due date approached, and my child showed no signs of arrival, my doctor demanded that I be induced the following week. After a few hours of contractions, I finally dilated to

8 cm and was ready to push. Within minutes, my beautiful angel was born. She was a dream. Excited, yet scared to be a mother of 3, I was ready to take my child home to unite her with her brother and sister whom impatiently awaited her arrival. Their paternal grandmother flew to Texas from California once again to assist. My children were blessed to have active paternal grandparents who genuinely loved and supported them.

Soon after my daughter was born, my fiancé and I decided to give our relationship another try. How did I allow him to come back into my life after all that he had put me through? We were still living in separate homes as we tried to make a toxic relationship work. Deep down, I knew it wouldn't work. His sneaky ways began catching up with him, as his other woman exposed her feelings for him. Eventually, the moment came where the other woman and I spoke over the phone. During that conversation, she told me that she was pregnant with his child. Shocked and hurt, but careful not to expose my emotions, we decided to call my children's father on 3 way. He disrespected her, as I sat on the phone silently smiling at the sound of pain in her voice. She had contributed to the pain I felt all those years, and it was her turn to cry. She eventually terminated her pregnancy at her own will.

Despite the emotional rollercoaster our relationship had been on, we began focusing more on our business again. We were saving all of our money on expansion. Eventually, we purchased two vehicles to add to our fleet, a black Mercedes Sprinter and a black presidential SUV. As energy into our business increased, we began manifesting amazing things. We were catering to some of the top celebrities in the world, from reality television stars to "the greatest rapper alive". Business with elite clientele became more frequent; we felt unstoppable. We had a business account, but weren't quite comfortable with having a large amount of cash sitting in the bank, so we decided to stash the money in a storage unit. This was a terrible decision! One day, he visited our storage unit to make the gut wrenching discovery of an empty unit. The bag that held almost $70,000 in it was gone. Feeling like I was in the twilight zone, I dropped to the floor as I sat on the phone with my children's father while he questioned what happened to the money. Later on, we discovered that he had accidentally left the unit unlocked after leaving in a rush one day. This day felt like one of the longest of my life. We had less than $20,000 dollars to our name and felt devastated. Experiencing financial losses had become a bit normal for us due to the various ones we faced over the years.

I no longer wanted to renew the lease to my house, so I decided to move into my child's father's house, temporarily. He wanted to maintain his ability to have space when he desired, meaning he wanted to experience the benefits of having a woman without having to fully commit. I didn't care, as I continued to be the best woman to him. Tensions were high as we were emotional over the loss, which resulted in us having one of the biggest fights of our relationship. He bruised my face with a black eye, a busted lip, and lumps throughout my head. I wasn't physically strong enough to defend myself, so I grabbed pepper spray and sprayed aimlessly, forgetting that my infant daughter was in the room. Luckily, she was unharmed.

Over the years, I had begun to reciprocate the abuse I endured. So, when faced with the potential of a fight, I rarely took steps to defuse the situation. He was physically abusive because he was stronger; I was mentally abusive because I knew the perfect words to fuel his anger. In an attempt to move past the fight, we began to shift our focus back into business. Making money together was the one thing we seemed to do well together. After slowly building our finances again, we decided that putting our money into real estate investments was the best move. We found property sitting on approximately 5 acres of land and purchased it, although this deal canceled out as closing day approached due to the seller not having proper identification.

One day, as we left our child with a babysitter, our infant daughter fell off the bed, resulting in her breaking her femur bone. Since my children's father and I were not present, we had no knowledge as to what really happened, resulting in inconsistencies with our story. Once CPS became involved, we were facing the possibility of losing custody of our 3 children. As the weeks passed, the pressure we felt intensified. Luckily, by the grace of God, the cameras that my children's father had in his home showed how my daughter fell off the bed. The footage saved us from losing our children. Everyone who knew me, knew the devoted mother I was, which made it shocking to know I was dealing with a CPS case. After full cooperation, CPS eventually closed the case with a letter confirming the dismissal of child abuse allegations. Though relieved, my kids' father and I were exhausted with the year's experiences thus far. We no longer felt comfortable in the home our daughter broke her leg in, so he moved out and into another condo; I moved into my own house.

Living in close proximity to each other, it seemed as if it became harder to separate completely. It was clear he had no intention of being the man I desired. He had proposed to me 4 years ago and I still hadn't become his wife. I now believed he never had intentions of marrying me, although he insisted his reason for losing interest in marriage was because I lost my engagement ring. After a while, I became exhausted battling the other woman over him, which resulted in me agreeing to the last option I thought would save my relationship. We began a 3-way relationship with the other woman, but it only lasted a week. That week was one of the most confusing experiences of my life. In the beginning, I felt satisfied but as days went by I woke up feeling like I had completely lost control of my life. I witnessed the man I loved for over 10 years, be affectionate and loving towards a woman that he betrayed me with. During the polygamous triangle relationship, he was always making sure that I understood despite the situation, I was the only one he was in love with, but I thought, how could that be so? After spending the week at his home, one morning, I got up and looked over at them in total disgust. Unable to bear the sight of the drastic turn my life had taken, I rushed to leave. Sensing something was wrong, he followed me home. In my room, I broke down crying like I had never before. I was broken. I was tired of the unhealthy love I had received from him all those years. I knew he couldn't love me properly, because he didn't know how to. I was giving a job to a man who wasn't qualified.

During this time, I hadn't been communicating properly with my family. Out of all my sisters, Vickey knew me the best. She had not heard from me in the past few days, and sensed something was wrong. She sent me a random, yet timely text expressing her concern. I assured her that I was fine but eventually broke down, explaining all the turmoil I had recently been a part of. Without judgement, she listened and offered her insight on the situation.

After we hung up the phone, she encouraged me to attend an event about real love, hosted by a well-known life coach, author, and speaker. The next day, I walked into the event ready to begin my healing journey, even in the midst of my children's father being disappointed with me for going without him.

As the first self-help seminar I had ever attended, it was the most powerful event I had witnessed. This day, I made a promise to myself to leave the toxic relationship with my middle school sweetheart of 13 years. I walked away from my business, the property we acquired, and all the money we had saved. I left with $9,700, the rest of my dignity and self-love. I immediately began my healing journey as I focused on building the only relationship I needed at the moment - God. I knew with all I had endured, he was the only one who could reach the depths of my heart that needed to be healed.

Part III

*N*ot even a month after my man and I moved into our new apartment, I woke up one morning with the instinct to look in his phone. We had a very healthy relationship and trusted each other completely; however, my intuition had been sensing that something was wrong. Every time I had asked him how he was feeling, he said everything was fine. I knew he wasn't. He had just experienced one of his closest family member's death. This was also the first time he would be living on his own, which brought a level of financial responsibility I was very familiar with. I couldn't resist the urge, so once he got in the shower, I picked up his smartwatch and began to scroll through text messages. Upon clicking on the first text, I couldn't believe my eyes! The love of my life, the man I planned on breaking multiple generational curses with, had been casually texting another woman the day before. I ran outside to take a drive down the street and continued to conduct my research. He hadn't noticed his watch was missing and while I was gone, he responded to her unanswered text from the previous night. Once I got back in the house, I began packing up my items in our apartment. I was hurt but more than anything, upset. How dare he text another woman the same day he expressed his excitement about marrying me? We had spent the last two years pouring value into each other's lives. I hated the thought of walking away from a person I had attempted to mold into my dream man. I'd always been clear on what I wanted and wouldn't tolerate in a relationship. Cheating, even if only in the form of casual text flirting, was non-negotiable. Of course, I broke up with him.

We talked over the next few days and I analyzed everything going on in his life that led up to his actions. Instead of lashing out like a crazy woman, I sought to understand why he behaved the way he did. I didn't want to internalize his behavior as a reflection of who I was as a woman. I knew who I was and what I brought to our relationship. His lack of honesty, poor judgement, and inability to cope with his current pain led to him texting another woman - he sought out an escape of what was going on in his personal life. I didn't excuse his behavior at all; instead, I forgave him for my own healing and growth. I was hurt and upset but surprisingly, handled the situation well. I didn't seek revenge; instead, I sought understanding, forgiveness and healing. My level of maturity in handling such a delicate situation allowed him to begin the journey of his own healing. He instantly sought out help towards strengthening the relationship he had been building with God for the last two years to help him cope with his pain.

I thought my now ex-man and I would have been preparing to be engaged soon; those thoughts were confirmed when he surprised me with a diamond store date to figure out my engagement ring size and style. I will never forget the joy I felt in my heart as I tried on my favorite pear-shaped rings in Tiffany's. I was excited about the thought of becoming a wife. However, even while ring shopping, I was no longer interested in building a life with him; my attention was now focused on completely healing from all the trauma I was born into, and rebuilding my own life, without him. I realized he was the same man who had lied to me about his age when we first met… the same man who emotionally cheated on me two years later. He was still a decent guy though, as he had changed drastically for me and the quality of his life had upgraded. I stuck with my decision of ending our relationship and vowed to never attempt to change a man ever again, no matter how good the intentions.

Although my healing journey had begun the moment I rededicated my life to Christ during college years, I had never confronted the deep pain I felt from my toxic childhood or the lack of love felt by my father. I just continued to move through life hurt, trying new things to ease the pain. I ran from stability, commitment and structure - not knowing those were a part of the solutions to my pain. I also allowed the wrong men into my life. Nonetheless,

I truly believe that all things have worked together for my good, from birth until now. I no longer regret any decisions I've made. I am highly confident that I am currently on the path toward a very promising future. As a woman of faith, I believe God has allowed me to undergo certain life events for a specific purpose. My life's pain has birthed my purpose.

CHAPTER 6

Sis, Heal

CHAPTER 6

Sis, Heal

A Healing Message From Francine

*A*lthough I stayed in situations longer than I should have, I never gave up on myself. I knew I was better than my current circumstances. There were times when I felt disappointed in myself for the life I was living because I knew I deserved better, and so did my kids.

One of the most important things you have to do is to forgive yourself for the pain that you caused yourself! Next, forgive the person who caused you pain even if they never ask for your forgiveness. When we allow someone to hurt us, it's our responsibility to do the proper work to heal. Yes, they hurt you and it's natural to feel like you want them to suffer. So in return, you tell them constantly how they hurt you, not realizing that you suffer when you stay in victim mode. It's never too late to learn from the mistakes of your past. Also, it's important to understand that the people that hurt you, were probably hurting. No, it's not an excuse but it's enough to forgive them. In order to open up room in your life to receive the good that God has in store for you, you have to free up space and rid your life of past pain. Hurt people, hurt people - it's cliché but it's true. I've forgiven my children's father for the pain he caused while we were in a relationship. With time, I was able to understand that he was suffering from his own traumatic past events that he had not yet healed from. Despite our past, I love my children's father and the family we created. I appreciate the years we shared, good and bad because it contributed to the woman I am today. My healing comes from sharing my story. My father was another person that I had to forgive in order to move forward in life. Although he wasn't present during my childhood years, he continues to make small efforts in being a supportive father now

When I finally made the decision to press forward and begin my healing process, I became intentional about building my relationship with God, praying constantly, hiring a life coach, and continuously feeding my brain with positive messages. Although every person's healing process is different, two things you must do is be intentional and stay consistent. You also have to understand that you can't do it alone. Thankfully, I've made it this far with the help of God, my children's love, my life coach, my sister Vickey, and other siblings. Healing is an everyday process that I face, and I'm thankful that my children can reap the benefits of my journey and witness their mother thrive and strive towards greatness. If I can begin to heal from a life filled with daddy issues, mommy issues, instability, homelessness, dangerous soul ties, illegal lifestyles, and toxic relationships, there is nothing that you can't heal from. You owe it to yourself and the generations that will come after you. You got this sis, heal!

A Healing Message From Victorian

As you've read our story, you may have felt aches in your heart, thinking about the man who sexually or physically abused you; the parent, child, sibling, or other close family member who passed away - the divorce, your abortion, being cheated on, and losing your job, business, or home. As time has passed since the event(s) occurred, what actions have you taken to address your pain in a healthy way? While we all handle pain differently, we owe it to ourselves and future families to begin the process of healing. Your healing has the power to break any chains or generational curse over your current or future family. Since pain is an inevitable part of life, there will always be some person or events that we must heal from. Healing is a life-long journey. Whether you decide to write a book, attend a seminar, go to church, sign up for counseling/therapy, or hire a life coach, it is wise to always be working on your healing process. There are levels of life waiting to receive the healed version of you. Don't hold yourself back. Forgive him. Forgive her. Forgive them. Forgive yourself. Move forward, persevere, and thrive. Sis, heal.

www.ingramcontent.com/pod-product-compliance
Lightning Source LLC
LaVergne TN
LVHW091157080426
835509LV00006B/730